GENDER EQUALITY AND SOCIAL INCLUSION ANALYSIS TO INFORM ADB'S COUNTRY PARTNERSHIP STRATEGIES AND PROJECT DESIGNS IN SOUTH ASIA
A GUIDANCE NOTE

DECEMBER 2023

ASIAN DEVELOPMENT BANK

ADB

Contents

Tables, Figures, and Boxes

Abbreviations

ADB	Asian Development Bank
CGA	country gender assessment
CPA	country poverty assessment
CPS	country partnership strategy
CSO	civil society organization
DFID	Department for International Development of the United Kingdom
DMC	developing member country
GAP	gender action plan
GESI	gender equality and social inclusion
GESIDSS	GESI diagnostic of selected sectors
HPSA	Handbook on Poverty and Social Analysis
IPSA	initial poverty and social analysis
LNOB	leave no one behind
NRM	Nepal Resident Mission
OP	operational priority
SARD	South Asia Department
SOGIESC	sexual orientation, gender identity and expressions, and sexual characteristics
SPRSS	summary poverty reduction and social strategy

CHAPTER 1
Introduction

A. Purpose of this Guidance Note

1.   This guidance note presents approaches and tools for conducting a gender equality and social inclusion (GESI) analysis in six developing member countries (DMCs) of the Asian Development Bank (ADB) in South Asia. It is an accompanying material of the GESI framework that the ADB South Asia Department (SARD) developed to guide its application of the first two operational priorities of ADB Strategy 2030 in South Asia—operational priority 1 (OP1) is "addressing remaining poverty and reducing inequalities," and operational priority 2 (OP2) is "accelerating progress in gender equality."[1] The two Operational Priorities expand ADB's previous commitments as stated in OMC1/BP on poverty reduction (2004), OMC2/BP on Gender and Development (2010), and OMC3/BP Incorporation of Social Dimensions into ADB operations (2010). The GESI framework has seven key areas of action.[2] This guidance note serves to guide the implementation of its first two key areas of action: (i) informing country strategies and programs through GESI diagnostic of selected sectors, and (ii) strengthening project design through enhancing the quality of social and gender analysis and the GESI action plan.[3]

2.   The approaches and tools in this guidance note are for two levels of GESI analysis: (i) the country level to inform the GESI sections of ADB's country partnership strategies (CPSs), and (ii) the program or project level to define the GESI features of ADB-financed programs and projects. The intended users are the ADB SARD GESI teams, project teams, resident missions, and the executing and implementing agencies of ADB-financed projects.

---

[1]   ADB. 2018. *Strategy 2030: Achieving a Prosperous, Inclusive, Resilient, and Sustainable Asia and the Pacific.* Manila.
[2]   Before proceeding to the next sections of this guidance note, readers are advised to read the SARD GESI framework. The definitions of related key concepts, including groups affected by inequality, exclusion, vulnerability, and intersectionality, are included in the SARD GESI framework and hence are not repeated here.
[3]   The seven key areas of action of the SARD GESI framework are (i) informing country strategies and programs, (ii) strengthening GESI in project design, (iii) engaging in GESI law and policy reform, (iv) developing the capacity of partner agencies in delivering GESI results, (v) partnering with other social development actors, (vi) capturing GESI progress and results, and (vii) investing in GESI-relevant knowledge.

Gender Equality and Social Inclusion Analysis to Inform ADB's Country Partnership Strategies
and Project Designs in South Asia

2

3.   The focus of the GESI analysis is on individuals and groups that are excluded and vulnerable because of their gender; age; disability; social identity (e.g., ethnicity, caste, or religion); sexual orientation, gender identity and expression, and sexual characteristics (SOGIESC); income status; geographic location; or migrant status. Special attention is on women, girls, and other individuals and groups experiencing overlapping discrimination because of the intersection of these dimensions in their lives. This intersectionality lens, also discussed in the Strategy 2030 Operational Plan for OP 2, is highlighted in the SARD GESI framework as a guiding concept.[4]

B.   Gender Equality and Social Inclusion Analysis: Definition

4.   In this guidance note, GESI analysis refers to the identification of the excluded and vulnerable people [or persons, groups] in the country (for CPSs) or project areas (for program or project designs) and the systematic examination of (i) their conditions (social, economic, and political issues); (ii) the barriers to their access to and control over social, economic, and political resources, assets, and opportunities; (iii) their collective agency and capacity (i.e., to claim their rights, access available development resources and opportunities, and link to service providers); and (iv) the initiatives—e.g., policies, structures, programs, projects, and activities—to address these issues and barriers, unleash their agency, and develop their capacity. The analysis uses the three pillars of the Leave-No-One-Behind (LNOB) framework of the Department for International Development of the United Kingdom (DFID), now the Foreign, Commonwealth and Development Office (para. 10).

C.   ADB's Gender Equality and Social Inclusion Analytical Frameworks: Overview of Current Practice

5.   This guidance note builds on and supplements the social and gender analytical frameworks and procedures in ADB's Handbook on Poverty and Social Analysis (HPSA), developed in 2012.[5] Similar to the HPSA, this note does not propose additional policies and procedural requirements for conducting a GESI analysis for CPSs and programs or projects. Instead, this note presents approaches and tools—in line with ADB's existing policies and current requirements—for sharpening the analysis of intersecting inequalities experienced by women and excluded and vulnerable groups in South Asia, and integrating the results in CPSs and project designs.

---

4   ADB's Strategy 2030 OP2 Operational Plan for OP2, para. 43 states, "The SDG 'leave no one behind' principle requires DMCs to address discrimination against and disadvantages for women, including those related to class, ethnicity, indigenous, sexual orientation and gender identity, disability, religion, age, and migration." In SARD's GESI framework, intersectionality is defined as an analytical lens that describes the extent of inequality, exclusion, and vulnerability (or power and advantage) that individuals or groups experience by examining how their different identities intersect or overlap. An intersectional perspective is essential to show that women and girls are not homogenous groups but people experiencing different levels of disadvantage and disempowerment (or advantage and power) depending on their intersecting identities. The term was coined by Kimberlé Crenshaw to explain the oppression experienced by African-American women. She defined it as "a way in which multiple forms of inequality or oppression (such as racism, sexism, classism, ableism, heterosexism, and more) can compound and create different modes of discrimination or disadvantage." K. Crenshaw. 1989. Demarginalizing the Intersection of Race and Sex: A Black Feminist Critique of Antidiscrimination Doctrine, Feminist Theory and Antiracist Politics. *University of Chicago Legal Forum.* Vol. 1989, Article 8.
5   ADB. 2012. *Handbook on Poverty and Social Analysis: A Working Document.* Manila. This Handbook is being reviewed and updated.

Guide for Analysis to Inform Country Partnership Strategies

6.   ADB develops a CPS for each DMC every 3 to 5 years. As guided by the HPSA, each CPS includes an overview of issues and challenges on GESI in the country and has a section on ADB's strategy or priority actions to address these issues. A CPS includes an overview of gender issues and challenges in the country and specifies how ADB intends to promote and implement its overall gender equality and women's empowerment objectives in that DMC. In SARD, the practice is to expand the CPS's sections on gender analysis and gender strategy to GESI analysis and GESI strategy to include the issues and challenges faced by other disadvantaged groups in the country, such as older people, people with disabilities, social identity groups, people with diverse SOGIESC, income poor people, and people in difficult geographic locations, especially those experiencing overlapping discrimination due to their intersecting disadvantaged identities, and ADB's planned actions for their empowerment and inclusion.[6] As guided by the HPSA, to prepare the GESI sections of a CPS, ADB conducts three diagnostics and the strategies for addressing poverty and social issues in a CPS. It has a comprehensive list of tools (e.g., institutional analysis, stakeholder analysis, client or beneficiary assessment, poverty impact analysis) with clear specifications if these tools are to be applied at the country, sector, and/or project levels. The HPSA also provides a comprehensive list of qualitative and quantitative data collection methods, which continue to be relevant and useful for ADB Strategy 2030 operationalization. However, while gender and poverty assessments are explicit in the HPSA, the definitions and approaches related to intersecting inequalities, exclusion, and vulnerability are less explicit. For this reason, this guidance note aims to supplement the HPSA.

ADB South Asia Department's Practice in Gender Equality and Social Inclusion Analysis for Country Partnership Strategies

7.   In SARD, the CPA, CGA, and sector assessments are merged in the GESI diagnostic of selected sectors (GESIDSS), which it conducts for each DMC every 3 to 5 years. This practice was initiated by the Nepal Resident Mission (NRM) with its simultaneous focus on GESI in line with the country's national policy agenda and programs. ADB Strategy 2030 OP1 and OP2 have provided SARD with the impetus to expand NRM's practice to SARD's other DMCs.

Guide for Analysis to Inform the Gender Equality and Social Inclusion Features of Programs and Projects

8.   ADB has established procedural requirements for conducting poverty and social analysis, including gender analysis, at the project concept and design phases and monitoring and reporting the poverty and social dimensions of a project's progress and results. At the project concept phase, which is the first phase of project preparation after CPS formulation, the ADB project team conducts a preliminary poverty and social analysis (PSA), including a preliminary gender analysis. The preliminary PSA and gender analysis involve collecting and analyzing data and information

---

[6]   The CPA includes (i) "disaggregation of poverty data by sex and other social factors, and inclusion of information on non-income indicators of poverty, gender inequalities, and marginalized groups in the poverty profile;" and (ii) "gender inequalities and social exclusion in the analysis of the causes of poverty" (footnote 5, p. 15). The CGA includes an analysis of the (i) "gender dimensions of poverty and inequality;" and (ii) "intersections between gender and other social factors, such as ethnicity/caste, age, or marital status" (footnote 5, p. 15). Furthermore, one of the key questions asked in sector assessments is "How do poverty and social factors, such as gender, ethnicity/race/caste, age, marital status, citizenship, urban/rural location, or disability, affect people's access to goods and services, resources, economic opportunities, information, and/or decision-making in the sector?" (footnote 5, p. 13).

disaggregated by sex or gender and other relevant social categories regarding people in the project areas.[7] The results will inform the project's preliminary gender and poverty reduction and social inclusion categorizations based on the project's preliminary design and monitoring framework (DMF). During the project design phase, the project team conducts in-depth PSA, including gender analysis, to validate the results of the preliminary PSA and gender analysis and finalize the project's DMF. Based on the final DMF, the project team confirms the project gender categorization[8] and poverty reduction and social inclusion categorization.[9]

ADB South Asia Department's Practice in Gender Equality and Social Inclusion Analysis for Programs and Projects

9. Long before the effective date of ADB Strategy 2030, with its equal attention to the pursuance of GESI, NRM had consolidated its analysis of gender and social issues and needed actions. Hence, NRM's project GAPs are called GESI action plans. In its GESI framework, SARD expands this practice to its other DMCs, hence consolidating the analyses and actions pertaining to Strategy 2030 OP1 (social inclusion) and OP2 (gender equality) to sharpen its analysis of intersecting inequalities and to strengthen its actions to achieve GESI results. Hence, in SARD DMCs, Gender Assessment and Action Plans (GAAPs) are often referred to as GESI action plans (GESIAPs) which follow standard bank-wide GAAP templates.

---

[7] ADB's Corporate Results Framework and gender mainstreaming guidelines require the disaggregation of data by sex (male-female). In South Asia, particularly in four DMCs (Bangladesh. Bhutan, India, and Nepal), which legally define gender identity as non-binary, data disaggregation may go beyond the binary sex (male-female) to include people with diverse SOGIESC. The other social categories that may be relevant to a project include age, disability, social identity, income status, and geographic location (e.g., rural/urban, upland/lowland, and disaster-prone/relatively safe to disaster).

[8] ADB's four-tier gender categorization system defines the extent of gender features in a project's design. At the highest level is the gender equity theme (GEN) category, where the project's design and monitoring framework (DMF) has at least one gender performance indicator at the outcome level and at least one gender performance indicator in 50% of the DMF outputs. Next to GEN is effective gender mainstreaming (EGM), which is not required to have a gender indicator at the outcome level but should have at least one gender indicator in 50% of the DMF outputs. Each project categorized GEN and EGM, except for results-based or policy-based loans, is required to have a gender action plan (called a GESI action plan in some projects). After EGM is *some gender elements* (SGE), which has gender indicators in less than 50% of the DMF outputs. The last is no gender elements, which has no gender performance indicators in the DMF. All projects, including those that are categorized no gender elements, are required to integrate gender considerations in the project's social safeguards framework and/or plan. ADB. 2021. *Guidelines for Gender Mainstreaming Categories of ADB Projects.* Manila.

[9] The currently being revised poverty and social analysis approach is envisaged to include a project's categorization based on its impact on poverty reduction and social inclusion and the participation of disadvantaged groups, as reflected in its DMF.

CHAPTER 2

Gender Equality and Social Inclusion Analytical Framework of the ADB South Asia Department

10.   For its GESI analytical and action framework, SARD adopts DFID's LNOB framework, which is based on a core commitment of the United Nations Sustainable Development Goals to reach people who are furthest behind. Central to the agenda of the LNOB framework is the concept of intersectionality, which explains how identities (e.g., gender, age, disability, social identity) intersect to create overlapping and interdependent systems of discrimination or disadvantage.[10] The LNOB framework has three pillars: (i) understand for action, (ii) empower for change, and (iii) include for opportunity. Pillar (i) is focused on the analysis of the situation of the disadvantaged, and pillars (ii) and (iii) are guides for designing and evaluating responses. Table 1 presents SARD's definitions of these three pillars.

Table 1: Guide for Analyzing Issues and Designing Actions

Domains	Understand for Action	Empower for Change	Include for Opportunity
Purpose	Identify barriers to GESI and analyze the capacities of women and excluded and vulnerable groups to claim their rights and promote GESI based on disaggregated data and evidence	Promote the livelihood, voice, and social empowerment of women and excluded and vulnerable groups	Ensure the GESI-responsiveness of the social, political, and physical environment, including infrastructures, technologies, resources, and services
Questions for Analysis	• Who is excluded and vulnerable? • Why are they excluded and/or vulnerable? • What are the barriers to their access to services, resources, and opportunities? • What are their resources and capability in removing these barriers?	What laws, policies, institutional arrangements, strategies, programs, and projects contribute or can contribute to: • Livelihood and/or resource empowerment • Voice empowerment • Social empowerment (improving individual and collective social capital)	• Changing harmful formal and informal norms and practices • Making public infrastructures, facilities, spaces, workplaces, and services an enabling environment for GESI

GESI = gender equality and social inclusion.

Source: Asian Development Bank (South Asia Department), patterned from S. Herbert. 2019. Leaving No One Behind: Perspectives and Directions from DFID Multi-Cadre Conferences. *K4D Emerging Issues Report*. Brighton, United Kingdom: Institute of Development Studies.

---

[10] S. Herbert. 2019. Leaving No One Behind: Perspectives and Directions from DFID Multi-Cadre Conferences. *K4D Emerging Issues Report*. Brighton, United Kingdom: Institute of Development Studies.

11.   In line with the SARD GESI framework, the situational analysis under the first pillar focuses on the identified dimensions of exclusion and vulnerability in South Asia: gender, age, disability, social identity (minority ethnic groups and castes if present in the country or project areas), diverse SOGIESC, income status, geographic locations, and migrant status. The analysis has two parts (Box 1). The **first part is descriptive**, presenting their social, economic, and political conditions (including the interactions of the different dimensions of exclusion and vulnerability in their lives) and the barriers to GESI. The **second part is an in-depth analysis** of the immediate, intermediate, and structural causes of their exclusion and vulnerability, including the recognition that women in all groups experience higher exclusion.[11] **Immediate causes** (at the person or self and micro levels) are direct causes (e.g., lack of education or skills, lack of self-confidence, constraints on physical mobility, insufficient income, domestic violence, and others). **Intermediate causes** (at the meso level) are indirect factors that contributed to the situation (e.g., government's insufficient budget for childcare facilities, lack of programs to engage men and boys in gender equality, lack of funds for assistive technology and to improve the accessibility and safety of transportation infrastructures and facilities, lack of support programs for survivors of gender-based violence, and others). **Structural causes** are macro-level factors that have allowed the perpetuation of inequality, exclusion, and vulnerability across households, communities, organizations, workplaces, and public places over a long period (e.g., traditional gender norms that position men as the head of households and women as primarily responsible for household management and childcare, laws and policies that uphold the binary definition of sex and gender, laws and norms that tolerate the unequal distribution of assets, and others).

Box 1: Understand for Action—Gender Equality and Social Inclusion Analysis in Two Parts

First part: Descriptive
- Existing dimensions of inequality, exclusion, and vulnerability in the country or sector or project areas
- Social, economic, and political conditions of women and girls and excluded and vulnerable groups, including the interactions of the different dimensions of exclusion and vulnerability in their lives

Second part: In-depth analysis
- Immediate causes: Direct causes or factors (e.g., roles of men and women's multiple burden) that contributed to the situation of women and/or girls and excluded and vulnerable groups
- Intermediate: Indirect causes or factors (including people and institutions) that influenced the situation
- Structural: Factors that have allowed the perpetuation of gender inequality, social exclusion, and vulnerability across households, communities, organizations, workplaces, and public places over a long period

Source: Adopted from N. Kabeer and R. Subrahmanian. 1996. *Institutions, Relations and Outcomes: Framework and Tools for Gender-Aware Planning.* Sussex: Institute of Development Studies.

---

12.   In SARD's adaptation of the LNOB framework, while both the second and third pillars encompass laws, policies, institutional arrangements, and programs and projects, and aim to transform the situation of excluded and vulnerable groups, the focus of analysis and actions is different.

(i)   "Empower for change" is focused on analyzing and developing or strengthening their capacity to claim their right to social and economic resources, services, and opportunities; improve their livelihood;

---

[11]   Adopted from N. Kabeer and R. Subrahmanian. 1996. *Institutions, Relations and Outcomes: Framework and Tools for Gender-Aware Planning.* Sussex: Institute of Development Studies.

participate in decision-making and leadership or governance at different levels (e.g., family, community, organization, workplace, and local and national governance structures); and prepare and respond to disasters triggered by natural hazard. Areas for GESI analysis under this pillar are in Box 2.

(ii)   "Include for opportunity" is focused on analyzing and transforming the physical and social environment—systems, structures, norms, infrastructures, technologies, and practices—by making them inclusive or promotive of GESI. Areas for GESI analysis under this pillar are in Box 3.

Box 2: Empower for Change—Gender Equality and Social Inclusion Analysis in Two Parts

First part: Descriptive
- Existing laws, policies, key programs and/or schemes, and nodal agencies that aim to directly develop the livelihood and/or employment, voice, and social capital of women and excluded and vulnerable groups
- Main contents of these laws, policies, and programs and/or schemes
- Resources for the implementation of the laws, policies, and programs; networks and influencers that can be tapped to support supportive laws, policies, and programs

Second part: In-depth analysis of level of enforcement and outcomes
- Immediate and intermediate causes of enforcement or non-enforcement of laws and effectiveness or failure of policies and programs (e.g., weaknesses of the laws, policies, and programs; capacity of nodal agencies; active participation of civil society organizations)
- Immediate outcomes: changes in the livelihood, voice, and social capital of targeted groups
- Structural outcomes: Effects on the identified barriers to livelihood, voice, and social empowerment of women and excluded and vulnerable groups

Source: Asian Development Bank (South Asia Department).

Box 3: Include for Opportunity—Gender Equality and Social Inclusion Analysis in Two Parts

First part: Descriptive
- Existing laws, policies, key programs and/or schemes, and nodal agencies that aim to make the physical and social environment (e.g., educational and/or training facilities and curriculums, transportation infrastructures and facilities, accessibility of water and sanitation facilities, energy supply, and information and communication technologies) inclusive or promotive of gender equality and social inclusion
- Main contents of these laws, policies, and programs and/or schemes
- Resources allocated for the implementation of the laws, policies, and programs

Second part: In-depth analysis of level of enforcement and outcomes
- Immediate and intermediate causes of enforcement or non-enforcement of laws and effectiveness or failure of policies and programs (e.g., weaknesses of the laws, policies, and programs; capacity of nodal agencies; multi-stakeholder convergence; active participation of civil society organizations, including those of excluded and vulnerable groups; people and institutions that drive the exclusion)
- Immediate outcomes: e.g., gender equality and social inclusion features of schools, training institutes, infrastructures, and technologies, and increased number of women and girls and people from excluded and vulnerable groups benefiting from them
- Structural outcomes: e.g., shifts in social and gender norms on the use of infrastructures, facilities, and services by people of different social categories; inclusive education; smart and livable cities for all; and others

Source: Asian Development Bank (South Asia Department).

CHAPTER 3

Gender Equality and Social Inclusion Diagnostic of Select Sectors to Inform the Country Partnership Strategy

13. This section provides the components and contents—in line with the three pillars of the LNOB framework—of the GESI analysis of the national situation and each of ADB's sectors of engagement in each DMC in South Asia. The selection of specific sectors is based on the priority areas of collaboration between ADB and each DMC.[12] The methods for data collection and analysis are in paras. 29-33 of this guidance note. The results of the GESI analysis are presented in a GESIDSS report, which SARD conducts in each DMC every 3 to 5 years; the GESIDSS report forms the main reference for the GESI sections of the CPS.[13] The first chapter of the GESIDSS report is an overview of the national GESI situation. The succeeding chapters discuss the GESI situation in each selected sector. The concluding chapter summarizes the GESI issues that cut across the sectors and provides recommendations for ADB's and other development partners' possible areas of action.

14. The GESI analysis of the national situation and each sector has two common components: (i) the situation of women and excluded and vulnerable groups; and (ii) relevant policies, laws, institutions, and programs. The first component is in line with the "understand for action" LNOB pillar, while the second component is in line with the "empower for change" and "include for opportunity" pillars. The GESI analysis of each sector also includes a third component, which is the description of selected exemplary GESI practices of development players (governments, international development agencies, civil society organizations [CSOs], and private business organizations) in GESI mainstreaming in the sector.

A. Gender Equality and Social Inclusion Analysis of the National Situation: Components

The Situation of Women and Other Disadvantaged Groups in the Country

15. The key elements of this first component are in Box 1. For a sharper analysis or description of the manifestations of inequality, exclusion, and vulnerability in the country, the GESI analysis may adopt a modified form of Sara Longwe's Women's Empowerment Framework.[14] This framework looks at five levels of equality or

---

[12] ADB's engagement in a country may be in these sectors: (i) agriculture, natural resources, and rural development; (ii) education; (iii) energy; (iv) finance; (v) health; (vi) industry and trade; (vii) information and communication technology; (viii) public sector management; (ix) transport; and (x) water and other urban infrastructure and services.

[13] The results of the GESI analysis of each sector in the GESIDSS may also be used in helping the sector agencies develop their GESI strategy. See SARD's separate guidance note for developing the GESI strategy of sector agencies.

[14] C. March, I. Smyth, and M. Mukhopadhyay. 1999. *A Guide to Gender-Analysis Frameworks.* Oxford, United Kingdom: Oxfam GB.

empowerment. Its proposition is that the higher the level of equality in society, the higher the level of development and empowerment of women (Figure 1).

(i)   At the lowest level is **Welfare**, which refers to equality in the enjoyment of basic goods and services, such as food, water supply, sanitation facilities, medical care, education and training, and assistive devices for people with orthopedic, visual, and/or hearing impairment.

(ii)   The next level is **Access**, which refers to equality in access to or use of factors of production, such as land, labor or jobs, credit or capital for business, training, marketing facilities, and all available services and benefits.

(iii)   The third level is **Conscientization**, which refers to the extent of shifts from traditional beliefs or norms that cause gender inequality and social discrimination to an explicit recognition of the equal worth and rights of people regardless of sex, gender, age, disability, social identity, SOGIESC, income status, and geographic location. Being at the third level means that the recognition or change in mindsets is not enough, but that this shifting of perspectives should be reflected in the transformation of practices.

(iv)   **Participation** is in decision-making, policymaking, planning, and administration, as well as in all phases of, for instance, the project development cycle and other organizational components.

(v)   **Control** is not just participation in decision-making but also equal control over factors of production (land, labor, capital, entrepreneurship) and the distribution of their benefits without dominance or subordination.

Figure 1: Longwe's Women's Empowerment Framework

	Level of Equality	Level of Empowerment
Control		
Participation		
Conscientization	Increased Equality	Increased Empowerment
Access		
Welfare		

Proposition: To reach the higher or highest level of equality and empowerment, it is necessary to also work for the achievement of equality and empowerment at the lower levels.

Source: C. March, I. Smyth, and M. Mukhopadhyay. 1999. *A Guide to Gender-Analysis Frameworks*. Oxford, United Kingdom: Oxfam GB.

16.   Appendix 1 provides a list of questions to assess the national situation of women and excluded and vulnerable groups, and Appendix 2 provides examples of questions for the five levels of equality and development (para. 15).

Relevant Laws, Policies, Institutions, and Programs

17.   The objective of this second component is to look at the responses of major development players in the country (governments, international development agencies, CSOs, and private business organizations) to the analyzed situation of women and excluded and vulnerable groups in the country in general or across sectors. The analysis is in three types of response: (i) laws or policies, (ii) institutional or organizational operations, and (iii) programs and budget for GESI. The key elements of the analysis are in Box 2 and Box 3. To closely examine the contributions of laws, policies, institutions, and programs to GESI, particularly to "empower for change" and "include for opportunity," paras. 18-23 provide guides for analyzing each of them. Checklists of questions are in appendixes 3 and 4.

Laws and Policies

18.   To assess the contributions of existing laws and policies to GESI, particularly to "empower for change" and "include for opportunity," this guidance note proposes the use of a policy analysis framework that integrates the intersectionality lens. An intersectionality-based policy analysis framework is applicable for this analysis.[15] This intersectionality-based policy analysis has two core components: a set of 8 guiding principles that serve to define the focus or the themes and methodology of the analysis, and a set of 12 questions that will shape the analysis. Table 2 provides an interpretation of these principles. Appendix 5 presents the 12 questions.

Table 2: Guiding Principles of Intersectionality-Based Policy Analysis Framework

Principle	Meaning	Implications for Policy Analysis
1. Reflexivity	Policy analysis is influenced by the worldviews (beliefs), knowledge, roles, and social identities of the policy analysts.	• Policy analysts need to state how their worldviews and background can influence the policy analysis. • Policy analysts of different backgrounds need to engage in dialogues to identify their common ground and acknowledge their differences.
2. Diverse knowledge	Different stakeholders may have different perspectives on the policy. It is important to recognize this diversity and ensure that the perspectives and knowledge of women and excluded and vulnerable groups are heard.	• Involve different stakeholders, including women, men, and people with diverse SOGIESC, and other excluded and vulnerable groups. • Bring diverse perspectives and knowledge on the policy to the surface, and document these perspectives and knowledge. Amid diversity, search for common ground.
3. Intersecting categories	People cannot be reduced to singular and distinct categories, and policy analysis cannot assume the primary importance of any one social category. Instead, social categories interact with and co-constitute one another to create certain social conditions.	• The policy analysis has to examine the policy's recognition and response to the intersecting identities of the people whom it seeks to serve. For instance, recognize that the policy may have different outcomes on different groups of women, e.g., old and young, with and without disability, and from different ethnic groups and/or income groups in the urban and rural areas. • Assess the policy's contributions to the pillars of OP1 and OP2 and their GESI-related provisions.

continued on next page

---

[15]   O. Hankivsky et al. 2014. An intersectionality-based policy analysis framework: critical reflections on a methodology for advancing equity. *International Journal for Equity in Health.* 13 (119).

Table 2 continued

Principle	Meaning	Implications for Policy Analysis
4. Time and space	The condition of people and groups, which the policy seeks to serve, is not static or fixed, but fluid and changeable. Perspectives on their condition and on a policy's outcomes may also change over time depending on the analysts' changing social positioning or location, among other factors.	• Consider the policy analysis and the search for a transformative policy as a continuing process. • It is important to state the time and space or location—especially distinct conditions in the stated time and space—when the policy analysis was undertaken.
5. Multilevel analysis	The policy analysis needs to examine how the policy framed the problems at the immediate (micro), intermediate (meso), and structural (macro) levels and its solutions and/or actions at these different levels.	Ensure that the policy analysis covers the micro, meso, and macro levels.
6. Power	The analysis should examine how the policy addresses (or exacerbates) discrimination against certain groups. The policy analysis process should also ensure that the voices of different stakeholders, especially the excluded and vulnerable groups, are heard and that the principle of "power with others" (i.e., people working together as collective actors) is promoted.	An important focus of the policy analysis is on how it seeks to (i) remove or reduce discrimination against excluded and vulnerable groups or address or reinforce or reduce gender and social inequality, (ii) promote the participation of women and other disadvantaged groups, and (iii) identify how male engagement (to reduce gender inequalities) is integrated as an approach.
7. Social justice	A policy should promote the recognition and respect for rights of people and groups regardless of gender, age, disability, social identity, SOGIESC, income, and geographic location.	An important focus of the policy analysis is on how the policy promotes the recognition and respect for rights of people, especially the excluded and vulnerable people [or persons, groups].
8. Equity	Equity is concerned with fairness. A policy should seek to equalize outcomes between more and less advantaged groups.	An important focus of the policy analysis is on how the policy promotes affirmative actions for disadvantaged groups (women and girls and excluded and vulnerable groups, especially those experiencing overlapping discrimination because of their intersecting disadvantaged identities) toward achieving GESI.

GESI = gender equality and social inclusion; OP1 = operational priority 1; OP2 = operational priority 2; SOGIESC = sexual orientation, gender identity and expression, and sexual characteristics.

Sources: The Asian Development Bank South Asia Department's interpretation of the intersectionality-based policy analysis. O. Hankivsky et al. 2014. An intersectionality-based policy analysis framework: critical reflections on a methodology for advancing equity. *International Journal for Equity in Health*. 13 (119); and O. Hankivsky et al. 2012. *An Intersectionality-Based Policy Analysis Framework*. Vancouver: Institute for Intersectionality Research and Policy, Simon Fraser University.

19.   The principles of the intersectionality-based policy analysis framework apply to the analysis of institutions and programs and budgeting. Other considerations are in paras. 20 and 21.

Institutional Analysis

20.   The institutional analysis begins with identifying the nodal agencies responsible for promoting GESI and the pillars of OP1 and OP2 of Strategy 2030. In analyzing the extent to which GESI is mainstreamed in the nodal agencies, this guidance note suggests to use a modified form of the analytical framework developed by the international feminist network Gender at Work.[16] This framework describes an organization with four dimensions

---

[16]   A. Rao, D. Kelleher, and C. Miller. 2015. No Shortcuts to Shifting Deep Structures in Organisations. *Institute of Development Studies Bulletin*. 46 (4).

Gender Equality and Social Inclusion Analysis to Inform ADB's Country Partnership Strategies
and Project Designs in South Asia

12

(Figure 2). SARD has modified the description of each quadrant to also integrate social inclusion. The top two quadrants are concerned with individuals, especially women and people belonging to disadvantaged groups (e.g., people with disabilities, people with diverse SOGIESC, and minority social identity groups) in the institution. The top right quadrant is about their equal access to the institution's resources (e.g., equal wage for work of equal value, career development, and promotion) and the GESI sensitivity of their services. The top left quadrant is about their understanding of their equal rights and capability to perform key roles, participate in decision-making, and assert their right to the resources and services of the institution. The bottom two quadrants are systemic, with

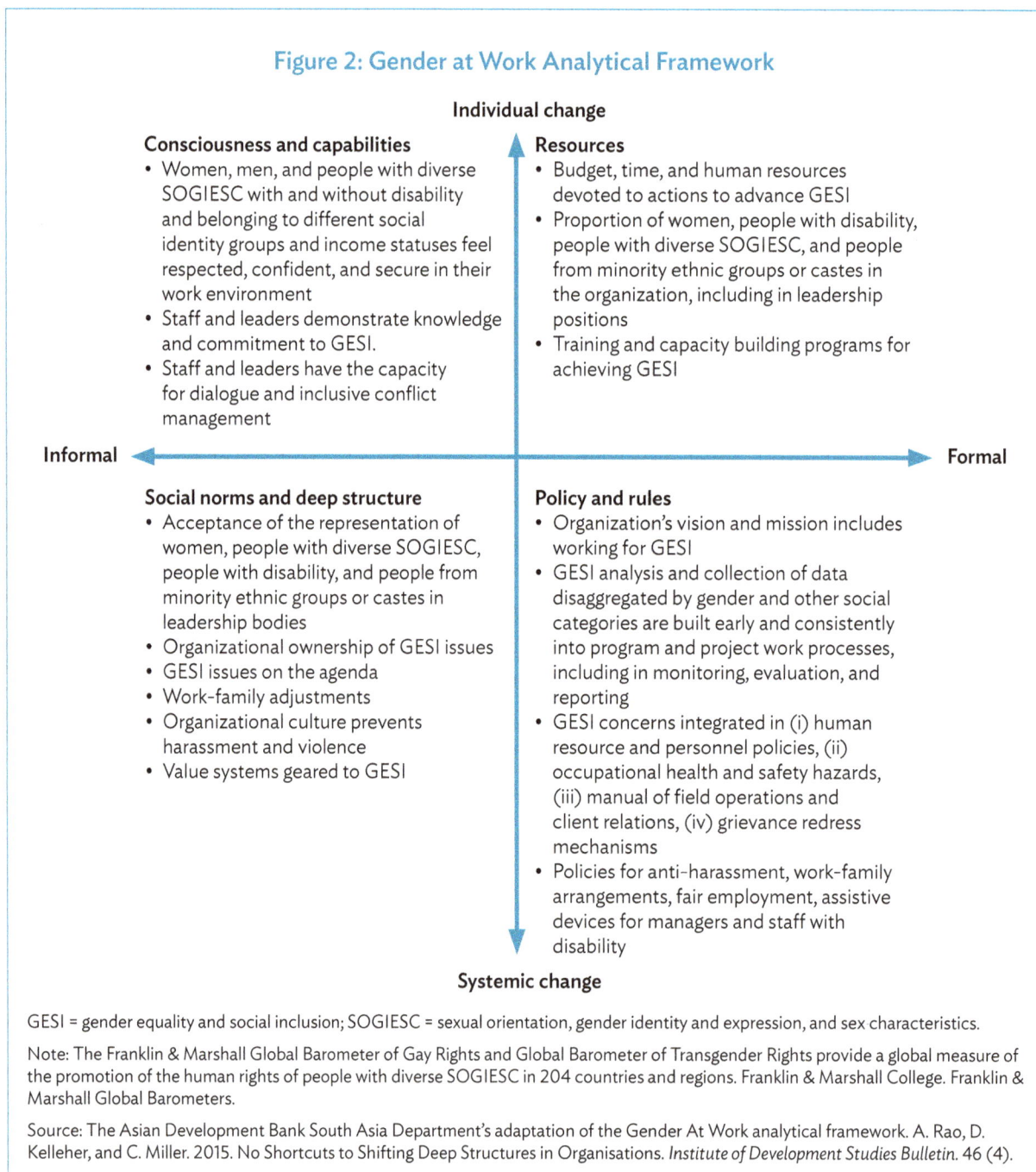

Figure 2: Gender at Work Analytical Framework

Individual change

Consciousness and capabilities
- Women, men, and people with diverse SOGIESC with and without disability and belonging to different social identity groups and income statuses feel respected, confident, and secure in their work environment
- Staff and leaders demonstrate knowledge and commitment to GESI.
- Staff and leaders have the capacity for dialogue and inclusive conflict management

Resources
- Budget, time, and human resources devoted to actions to advance GESI
- Proportion of women, people with disability, people with diverse SOGIESC, and people from minority ethnic groups or castes in the organization, including in leadership positions
- Training and capacity building programs for achieving GESI

Informal ← → **Formal**

Social norms and deep structure
- Acceptance of the representation of women, people with diverse SOGIESC, people with disability, and people from minority ethnic groups or castes in leadership bodies
- Organizational ownership of GESI issues
- GESI issues on the agenda
- Work-family adjustments
- Organizational culture prevents harassment and violence
- Value systems geared to GESI

Policy and rules
- Organization's vision and mission includes working for GESI
- GESI analysis and collection of data disaggregated by gender and other social categories are built early and consistently into program and project work processes, including in monitoring, evaluation, and reporting
- GESI concerns integrated in (i) human resource and personnel policies, (ii) occupational health and safety hazards, (iii) manual of field operations and client relations, (iv) grievance redress mechanisms
- Policies for anti-harassment, work-family arrangements, fair employment, assistive devices for managers and staff with disability

Systemic change

GESI = gender equality and social inclusion; SOGIESC = sexual orientation, gender identity and expression, and sex characteristics.

Note: The Franklin & Marshall Global Barometer of Gay Rights and Global Barometer of Transgender Rights provide a global measure of the promotion of the human rights of people with diverse SOGIESC in 204 countries and regions. Franklin & Marshall College. Franklin & Marshall Global Barometers.

Source: The Asian Development Bank South Asia Department's adaptation of the Gender At Work analytical framework. A. Rao, D. Kelleher, and C. Miller. 2015. No Shortcuts to Shifting Deep Structures in Organisations. *Institute of Development Studies Bulletin.* 46 (4).

the bottom right quadrant referring to formal rules that facilitate GESI and the bottom left quadrant relating to informal social norms and deep structures that shape the organization's gender and social culture, including power structures. In the institutional analysis, the general question is the extent to which GESI principles and practices are mainstreamed in the organization's functioning and results, as indicated by the presence of key GESI features in each quadrant of the Gender at Work Analytical Framework; some examples of which are in Figure 2.

Programs and Budgeting Analysis

21.   The framework for gender-aware planning of Kabeer and Subrahmanian may be expanded to include social inclusion concerns and used for GESI analysis of policies and programs and budget (footnote 11). This framework classifies a policy into two general categories, gender-blind and gender-aware, with the following definitions:[17]

(i)   "Gender-blind policy design and analyses are those which are implicitly premised on the notion of a male development actor and which, while often couched in apparently gender-neutral language, are implicitly male-biased in that they privilege male needs, interests and priorities in the distribution of opportunities and resources."

(ii)   "Gender-aware policy design and analyses, by contrast, recognize that development actors are women as well as men, that they are constrained in different and often unequal ways as potential participants and beneficiaries in the development process, and that they may consequently have differing and sometimes conflicting, needs, interests and priorities."

22.   Kabeer and Subrahmanian's framework further classifies gender-aware policies into three categories: (i) gender-neutral policies, which acknowledge gender issues and target the realization of related objectives but leave the existing divisions of resources, responsibilities, and capabilities intact; (ii) gender-specific policies, which focus on interventions for a group of women, like home-based income-generating projects; and (iii) gender-transformative policies, which target women or men or both and recognize the existence of gender-specific needs and constraints but additionally seek to transform the existing gender relations in a more egalitarian direction through the distribution of resources and responsibilities.

23.   To apply this framework to the GESI review of programs, the following is a reformulation of these definitions.

(i)   **GESI blind.** No explicit mention of GESI issues and actions addressing them; hence the program contributes to the status quo of persisting gender inequality and social exclusion, including the intersecting inequalities faced by women and girls of excluded and vulnerable groups.

(ii)   **GESI neutral.** Explicitly claims and/or assumes that all will benefit equally from the program or budget but without actions addressing the distinct empowerment and inclusion needs of excluded and vulnerable groups, especially women experiencing intersecting inequalities and vulnerabilities.

---

[17]   Footnote 11, pp. 2–3. Kabeer and Subrahmanian described gender-blind policies as the consequence of inappropriate assumptions and practices, one of which is the tendency to see women as a homogenous category with identical needs and interests. To explain, they cited an example of a failed project in India, "where government officials, noting that papad making was a 'female' activity in their locality, sanctioned a batch of loans to support papad making schemes for local women's groups. When the papad failed to sell, it was discovered that the women's groups belonged to scheduled caste households; members of other castes were not prepared to eat food made by them" (Footnote 11, p. 3). This statement suggests that Kabeer and Subrahmanian consider programs that are blind to the intersecting inequalities faced by some women as gender blind.

(iii) **GESI specific.** Aims to respond to the empowerment needs of women and excluded and vulnerable groups, especially women experiencing intersecting inequalities and vulnerabilities.

(iv) **GESI transformative.** Recognizes the specific empowerment and inclusion needs of women and each disadvantaged group (especially women of these groups) but also seeks to transform systems and structures (including social and gender norms) that create and perpetuate gender inequality and social exclusion.

B. Gender Equality and Social Inclusion Analysis of ADB's Sectors of Engagement

The Situation of Women and Other Disadvantaged Groups in Each Sector

24. The GESI analysis of each sector begins with identifying the manifestations of gender inequality and social exclusion in the areas of representation in relevant government sector agencies and private sector organizations, access to and control of its services and resources, and enjoyment of benefits. Appendix 6 provides two tables of questions that may help in this GESI analysis. Table A6.1 has questions that are applicable to all sectors, and Table A6.2 has questions for each specific sector. These questions supplement those in Box 1 of the ADB HPSA.[18]

25. **Relevant sector-specific laws, policies, institutions, and programs.** The GESI analysis of national and sector laws, policies, institutions, and programs is similar. Hence, the guides in Table 2, Figure 2, and paras. 21–23 are also applicable to the GESI analysis of sectors. In addition, the list of questions in Appendix 7 may also help.

26. **Good practices and lessons on gender equality and social inclusion mainstreaming in each sector.** In identifying good practices and lessons, these steps may be undertaken: (i) identify key programs of the government, CSOs, business organizations, and development partners that aim to benefit women and disadvantaged groups; (ii) state the GESI achievements of these programs, including their contributions to transforming social and gender norms; (iii) conduct an in-depth review of the successful and challenging experiences of these programs; and (iv) summarize the good practices, limitations, and lessons from these successful and challenging experiences, especially related to the pillars of OP1 and OP2. To select the most relevant good practice, tips in Box 4 may help.[19] Examples of questions to ask are as follows (detailed questions are in Appendix 8).

(i) What good practices and lessons emerge from implementing various policies that aim to enhance women's and disadvantaged groups' livelihood, empower their voice, and change discriminatory policies and mindsets?

(ii) Share in detail the good practice (content, design, implementation, and outcomes of the practice). Why is it considered a good practice? What methods and tools were used, and why were they effective? How did the intervention benefit the specific excluded or vulnerable group? How was it disseminated? How can its achievements be followed up and scaled up?

(iii) What are the key lessons? Why are they lessons? What was done well, and what needed improvement? Provide examples.

---

[18] Footnote 5, p. 13.
[19] Good practices may not be readily available for some disadvantaged groups, such people with diverse SOGIESC, as no impact evaluations have been done for most programs that aim to benefit them. Hence, the GESI analysis, in consultation with stakeholder groups, may explicitly say so.

Box 4: Tips on Selecting Good Practices in Gender Equality and Social Inclusion Mainstreaming

1. Select reasonably recent programs (in operation or concluded a year or so ago)
2. Select programs with some innovative component either in design or implementation to enable an understanding of good practices related to gender equality and social inclusion
3. Review any specific program highlighted by stakeholders during consultations or focus group discussions as having a significant impact, innovative features, or significant issues
4. Refer to secondary research to short-list exemplary programs

Source: Asian Development Bank (South Asia Department).

CHAPTER 4

Gender Equality and Social Inclusion Analysis to Inform the Gender Equality and Social Inclusion Features of Programs and Projects

27.   GESI analysis of programs and projects is primarily focused on women and excluded and vulnerable groups in the geographic location(s) of a program or project or its area(s) of influence. The results of the GESI analysis will define the program's or project's GESI design features (i.e., GESI outcome and output performance indicators and targets in the design and monitoring framework), set the baseline data of these indicators and targets, determine the program's or project's gender categorization, and design the GESI action plan if the program or project is categorized gender equity theme or effective gender mainstreaming.

28.   Questions for a program's or project's social and gender analysis can be found in ADB's HPSA (footnote 5). Other gender-related questions are in the ADB Operations Manual section on gender and development.[20] Appendix 9 provides additional questions in line with the three pillars of the LNOB framework and focuses on excluded and vulnerable groups in South Asia. Questions addressed to project beneficiaries and stakeholder groups are in Appendix 10.

---

[20]   ADB. 2010. Gender and Development in ADB Operations. *Operations Manual.* OM C2/BP. Manila.

CHAPTER 5
Guides for Data Collection and Analysis

29.   Most of the tools necessary for GESI analysis are provided in the ADB HPSA. The tools include gender analysis, institutional analysis, stakeholder analysis, conflict analysis, client or beneficiary assessment, socioeconomic profiling, poverty impact analysis, rapid participatory assessment, benefit incidence analysis, and risk and vulnerability profiling. Provided in paras. 30–34 are some common data collection and analysis methods.

A.   Data Collection

30.   The GESI analysis of the national situation, sectors, and programs and projects is based on reliable (i) secondary data from governments, international development agencies, CSOs, and reputable academic and research institutions; and (ii) primary data, particularly from field visits and consultations (through focus group discussions, key informant interviews, and in-depth interviews) with key stakeholder groups, including the target beneficiaries—women, men, girls, boys, and people with diverse SOGIESC of disadvantaged groups. Some guides for the collection of secondary and primary data are in paras. 31 and 32.

31.   **Secondary data collection.** The project team may systematically review and collate evidence on the situation and challenges experienced by women and the disadvantaged groups in a DMC or program or project areas by reviewing reports, research articles, and other publications of the government (official reports and publications), development partners (reports and strategy papers), civil society (opinion and situational analysis papers), and academic or research institutions (research articles and books). Secondary document review will involve, among others, collating documents on policies, laws, and regulatory framework for women and excluded and vulnerable groups from government archives and websites, development partner publications, and academic research papers. This is done to identify GESI-related policies, schemes, missions, and programs of relevant ministries, and to analyze the GESI responsiveness of their clauses, provisions, institutional mechanisms, and implementation modalities. Reliable secondary data may not be available or data gaps may exist, such as on people with diverse SOGIESC. Hence, the GESI analysis should rely on primary data collection.

32.   **Primary data collection.** Stakeholder consultations are crucial for determining and integrating the perspectives of a wide range of stakeholders (especially beneficiary women, men, and disadvantaged groups; and identity-based CSOs and service organizations involved in the issues of these beneficiaries) in the GESI analysis. Table 3 provides an overview of points to consider when planning and conducting stakeholder consultations. In addition, possible stakeholders to meet during interviews and consultations are suggested in Appendix 11. Data collection methods, including sampling framework and methods, must be rigorously designed to ensure representation of all groups and safe and ethical ways for the participants, particularly those (e.g., people with diverse SOGIESC) who have aspects of their identity that are criminalized or not legally recognized, and are heavily ostracized.

Gender Equality and Social Inclusion Analysis to Inform ADB's Country Partnership Strategies
and Project Designs in South Asia

18

Table 3: Considerations in Planning and Conducting Stakeholder Consultations

Type	Phases	Consultation Checklist	Mode of Consultation
Stakeholder consultations can be through KII and IDIs, which are appropriate for consulting high-level officials with limited availability or with women, disadvantaged groups, and other key informants (including men and boys) who may be hesitant to share in a group setting. Consultations may also be through FGDs and consultation workshops with 10–15 persons. Often, IDIs can bring out underlying norms and power structures and local and contextual situations.	Stakeholder consultations can take place in phases. The initial phase may include KIIs, IDIs, and FGDs, and the next phases can comprise consultation workshops	Checklists of points to discuss or guide questions should be customized to the stakeholders' position (service provider or beneficiary; government, nongovernment, or business). They should be formulated in simple and easy-to-understand language and answerable in not more than 1 hour for KIIs or 2 hours for IDIs, FGDs, or workshops. The reviewers should seek the informed consent of the participants by giving them clear information on the purpose of the data collection, the risks (if any), and the benefits; and clarifying that their participation is voluntary. Care must be taken to maintain confidentiality of data sources.	Checklists of points to discuss or guide questions should be customized to the stakeholders' position (service provider or beneficiary; government, nongovernment, or business). They should be formulated in simple and easy-to-understand language and answerable in not more than 1 hour for KIIs or 2 hours for IDIs, FGDs, or workshops. The reviewers should seek the informed consent of the participants by giving them clear information on the purpose of the data collection, the risks (if any), and the benefits; and clarifying that their participation is voluntary. Care must be taken to maintain confidentiality of data sources.

FGD = focus group discussion, IDI = in-depth interview, KII = key informant interview.

Source: Asian Development Bank (South Asia Department).

Box 5: General Tips for Gender Equality and Social Inclusion-Sensitive Consultation Workshops, Key Informant Interviews, and Focus Group Discussions

1. Conduct, wherever possible, consultations in the local language with the help of local staff who have the requisite local context and understanding of cultural sensitivities.
2. Frame open questions and ensure respectful discussions with sufficient probing to get insights with depth.
3. Schedule discussions and interviews to suit the timings of the women and the disadvantaged to be consulted. For example, it might be difficult for women to join consultations at certain times because of household responsibilities or safety concerns, and for poor people because of work pressures.
4. Conduct meetings with both women and men (separately or together as appropriate) to understand existing gender relations; prevalent power structures and masculinity norms; the role that men and boys play in perpetuating these norms; and the impact of these norms on the lives of women, girls, men, and boys.
5. Engage civil society organizations that can be important allies in carrying out consultations, given their in-depth knowledge of local context.
6. Ensure inclusive and accessible venues that include, for example, ramps, braille, clear signage, tactile support, sign language interpreters for people with disability, toilets with accessibility features such as wide doors for those in wheelchairs, for women, men, and transgender groups.
7. Ensure that the sample participants selected for individual interviews adequately reflect the diversity of stakeholders. Special attention should be paid to the inclusion of members experiencing intersecting inequalities (e.g., women with disabilities, older women, income poor from disadvantaged ethnic groups or castes).
8. Use visual tools for community-level discussions to map gender relations (labor, access, and control profiles).
9. Ensure privacy and confidentiality of views expressed by respondents for their protection.

Source: Asian Development Bank (South Asia Department).

33.   Examples of questions to ask during the consultations are in Appendix 2. Box 5 provides tips for conducting GESI-sensitive consultations, key informant interviews, in-depth interviews, and focus group discussions.

B.   Data Collation, Analysis, and Validation

34.   Examples of procedures for qualitative data collation, analysis, and validation are the following:[21]

(i)   Transcribing meeting notes based on predetermined templates (e.g., a Microsoft table or Excel sheet with three columns: (a) source of data, (b) statements uttered during the key informant interview or focus group discussion or consultation workshop, (c) theme of statements [based on prepared codes];

(ii)   Collating and organizing the transcribed notes based on prepared codes for the themes of statements, such as types of issues (e.g., micro, meso, macro), causes of issues (e.g., immediate, intermediate, structural), types of responses (understand for action, empower for change, include for opportunity);

(iii)   Summarizing the identified themes and subthemes as collated using the prepared codes and identifying the most frequently mentioned themes and subthemes and their bearers or sources; and

(iv)   Presenting the results of the thematic analysis of statements in consultation workshops (e.g., with government stakeholders, CSOs, ADB project teams, and ADB resident mission GESI team) for validation and discussion of way forward.

---

[21]   For more guides on how to collate, analyze, and validate collected quantitative and qualitative data, see ADB SARD. Forthcoming. *Evaluating the Gender Equality and Social Inclusion Impacts of ADB-Financed Projects in South Asia: A Guidance Note*. Manila.

CHAPTER 6

Integrating Gender Equality and Social Inclusion Analysis Results in Country Partnership Strategies and Project Design

35.   The final step is to integrate the results of the GESIDSS or the GESI analysis at the country and sector levels in the CPSs and the results of the GESI analysis in the program or project design documents. Table 4 provides guides on how GESI analysis results could be used in various areas of SARD operations.

Table 4: Guidance on Incorporating Results of Gender Equality and Social Inclusion Analysis in South Asia Department Programs or Projects

Stage	Guidance
Country partnership strategy	• Include in the country-at-glance section indicators tracking the GESI situation in the country. • Identify key developmental challenges, in addition to other challenges, from a GESI perspective and include an assessment of how the gains of development have been distributed for women and across various excluded and vulnerable groups. Use the findings and insights obtained from the situational assessment. • Include the findings and recommendations related to social inclusion, along with gender equality and women's empowerment, under the country's developmental context. Also, address the issues of intersectionality and male engagement. • Inform ADB's strategic priorities and objectives with the overall and sector GESI analysis. Reflect GESI aspects, too, in the priorities identified for the country partnership strategies, which should respond to the pillars of OP1 and OP2 as relevant. • Inform ADB's implementation strategy and priorities with the good practices and lessons learned from other international development agencies, national agencies, and sector agencies while working on GESI policies and programs. • Address the identified GESI-related knowledge gaps in the ADB's knowledge operations.
Program or project design	**The gender equality and social inclusion analysis should inform the project design features.** • **Report and recommendations of the President.** GESI analysis will serve as a baseline assessment for the poverty, social, and gender due diligence. Integrate the GESI analysis in the full text of the report and recommendation of the President. • **Project administration manual.** Integrate the GESI analysis findings, recommendations, good practices, and lessons learned in the sections devoted to GESI (e.g., "gender and social dimensions") and other relevant sections of the project administration manual. Integrate aspects that respond to the OP1 and OP2 pillars, promote male engagement for women's empowerment and gender equality, and address intersectional inequalities. • **Design and monitoring framework.** Embed GESI aspects in the outcomes and outputs of the project based on the analysis, and link to the OP1 and OP2 tracking indicators. Set realistic GESI targets drawing from the situational assessment of women and the disadvantaged groups, covering the SARD GESI framework analytical components of understand for action, empower for change, and include for opportunity.

continued on next page

continued on next page

Table 4 continued

Stage	Guidance
Program or project design	• **Gender equality and social inclusion action plan.** Use insights from the GESI analysis (e.g., barriers in access to basic services, situation of human development) to formalize desired GESI outputs, indicators, and targets, as well as the activities required to achieve these.
	• **Social safeguards framework and plan.** Integrate GESI analysis findings regarding indigenous peoples and the population requiring resettlement in the resettlement and indigenous peoples planning frameworks and plans.
	• **Stakeholder communication strategy.** The communication strategy should recognize, based on the GESI analysis findings, the communication channels and mediums most accessible for women and people of disadvantaged groups. The language, methodology, and timing should be adjusted according to the gender and socially differentiated needs of the stakeholders.
	• **Community awareness and participation plan.** The insights from the GESI analysis should inform who needs to participate and how their participation can be ensured. The analysis findings should also be used to develop differentiated strategies to improve the awareness of women and people from disadvantaged groups in the community.

ADB = Asian Development Bank, GESI = gender equality and social inclusion, IPSA = initial poverty and social analysis, OP1 = operational priority 1, OP2 = operational priority 2, SARD = South Asia Department, SPRSS = summary poverty reduction and social strategy.

Source: ADB (SARD).

APPENDIXES

APPENDIX 1: QUESTIONS FOR GENDER EQUALITY AND SOCIAL INCLUSION ANALYSIS OF THE NATIONAL SITUATION OF WOMEN AND OTHER DISADVANTAGED GROUPS

Strategy 2030	Questions to "Understand for Action"

OP1: Addressing remaining poverty and reducing inequalities	1. What is the poverty situation (income and non-income) in the country?
	  • What percentage of the population is living below the poverty line, disaggregated by gender; geographic location (rural-urban); age range (0–12, 13–18, 19–59, 60 and older); with and without disabilities; and ethnicity or caste (if any)?
	2. Who are the disadvantaged or excluded and vulnerable in the country?
	  • What is the population of older people—disaggregated by age range (60–65, 66–70, and older than 70); gender; and location (urban and rural)? What disadvantages do older people experience?
	  • What is the population of people with disability—disaggregated by types of disabilities (visual, hearing, orthopedic, learning, mental health); gender; age range (0–12, 13–18, 19–59, 60 and older); and location (urban and rural)? What disadvantages do people with disability experience?
	  • Are there ethnic groups or castes that have less access to services, resources, assets, and opportunities because of their (as a group) income status, geographic location, level of education, and/or social norms and stereotypes? If yes, who are they? What is their population, disaggregated by gender, age range (0–12, 13–18, 19–59, 60 and older) and location (rural and urban)? What disadvantages do these ethnic groups or castes experience?
	  • Are there disadvantaged youth? If yes, what is their population, disaggregated by gender, disability, income status (below or above poverty line), and geographic location (urban and rural)? What disadvantages do they experience?
	3. What are (i) the barriers to the disadvantaged groups' access to services, resources or assets, and opportunities and (ii) their collective capacity (organized action and networking) and coping mechanisms according to the analysis of the following?
	  • Organizations composed of or representing the disadvantaged groups
	  • Concerned government agencies
	  • Civil society organizations, including academic and research institutions
	  • International development agencies
	4. Who are the groups that exercise power and control over the welfare of women and disadvantaged groups? In what ways? What impact does this exercise of power and control have on the lives of women and disadvantaged groups? How do these powerful groups get impacted by the power they hold?

OP2: Accelerating progress in gender equality	1. What is the sex ratio in the country, disaggregated by age range (0–12, 13–18, 19–59, 60 and older) and geographic location? What is the cause, or what are the causes, of the imbalanced sex ratio (if any)? 2. Are there data about women disadvantaged due to their age, disability, social identity (e.g., ethnicity, caste, religion), sexual orientation and gender identity, income status, geographic location, and migration and about individuals with diverse SOGIESC? If yes, what is their population, disaggregated by age range, geographic location (urban and rural), and poverty status (income and multidimensional poverty)? What types of disadvantages do they experience? What examples of exclusion do they experience in key sectors (e.g., health, education, finance, transport, water and other urban infrastructure services, energy, agriculture and natural resources, and public sector management)? What is the extent of violence they experience? Is this violence committed by state or non-state actors?

continued on next page

Appendix 1 continued

Strategy 2030	Questions to "Understand for Action"
	3. What percentage of the households are headed by women, men, and individuals with diverse SOGIESC, disaggregated by income and non-income status (below and above poverty line; multidimensional poverty), with and without disabilities, and ethnicity or caste? 4. What is the country's Gender Development Index and what is its Gender Inequality Index, according to the latest UNDP Human Development Report? 5. What are the country's Global Gender Gap Index and subindexes (health and survival, educational attainment, economic participation and opportunity, and political empowerment), according to the World Economic Forum? 6. What proportions of women and girls, people with diverse SOGIESC, and men and boys have experienced gender-based violence in the past 3–5 years? 7. Based on data from points 1 to 6 of OP2, what are the key national gender issues? 8. What are the barriers to gender equality in access to and control over resources and opportunities and collective capacity of women and individuals with diverse SOGIESC to seek gender equality according to the following? • Women's groups or organizations or feminist organizations and other civil society organizations • Government agencies concerned • Academic and research institutions • International development agencies
Intersectionality	Based on answers to the questions raised for OP1 and OP2, what are the key GESI (economic, political, and sociocultural) issues experienced by women, girls, and individuals with diverse SOGIESC who are members of disadvantaged groups compared to issues experienced by men and boys of the same disadvantaged groups and women, girls, and LGBT+ of advantaged groups (e.g., no disabilities, belonging to dominant ethnic groups or castes, in relatively affluent areas)? What specific barriers to GESI do they experience? What are their coping mechanisms?

GESI = gender equality and social inclusion; LGBT+ = lesbian, gay, bisexual, transgender, and others; OP1 = operational priority 1; OP2 = operational priority 2; SOGIESC = sexual orientation, gender identity and expression, and sexual characteristics; UNDP = United Nations Development Programme.

Note: There may be questions for which reliable data are difficult to obtain. Hence, as is the practice in the GESI diagnostic of selected sectors, it is advisable to include only those questions where reliable, evidence-based answers are available (i.e., primary data from reliable representatives of stakeholders and/or secondary data from the government and international development agencies and empirical studies from academic and reputable research institutions.

Source: Asian Development Bank (South Asia Department).

APPENDIX 2: EXAMPLES OF QUESTIONS TO ASK WHEN ADAPTING SARA LONGWE'S WOMEN'S EMPOWERMENT FRAMEWORK FOR GENDER EQUALITY AND SOCIAL INCLUSION ANALYSIS

Level	Questions related to Operational Priorities 1 and 2, and Intersectionality
1. Welfare	**Health** 1. What are the primary causes of morbidity and mortality of women, girls, men, boys, and people with diverse SOGIESC, especially those belonging to disadvantaged groups (old age, disadvantaged youth, with disability, minority ethnic groups or castes, income poor, located in difficult geographic locations, and migrants)? 2. Are there services available to prevent or reduce or manage these morbidity and mortality causes? Are these services equally available to them? If not, what are the barriers to their access to these services? 3. Are there services available for survivors of harassment and violence? If yes, what are these services? **Finance** 1. What are the requirements for accessing the financial resources and services of financing institutions (banks, credit facilities, microfinance institutes) in the country or project areas? 2. Are women, men, and people with diverse SOGIESC, especially those belonging to disadvantaged groups, equally capable of fulfilling these requirements? **Education and Training** 1. Are women, men, and people with diverse SOGIESC, especially those belonging to disadvantaged groups, able to equally access education and training facilities and programs? 2. Do these education and training programs respond to their distinct needs and capabilities? If not, what are the barriers?
2. Access	1. Do women, men, and people with diverse SOGIESC especially those belonging to disadvantaged groups, have equal access to or can they use available resources (e.g., land, water supply and sanitation facilities, transport, energy, information, market facilities, agricultural technology)? 2. If not, what are the barriers? 3. Who defines who can access these resources?
3. Conscientization	1. Are there policies, programs, or measures to raise public awareness and acceptance of the equal rights and dignity of women, girls, men, boys, and people with diverse SOGIESC, especially those belonging to disadvantaged groups? 2. What institutions are involved in implementing these policies, programs, or measures? What institutions bar the implementation of these policies, programs, or measures? Why?
4. Participation	Are women, men, and people with diverse SOGIESC, especially those belonging to disadvantaged groups, equally able to participate in decision-making in different levels of society (households, community, organizations, workplace, government) and assume leadership positions?
5. Control	Are women, men, and people with diverse SOGIESC, especially those belonging to disadvantaged groups, able to control the distribution of benefits of resources and services?

SOGIESC = sexual orientation, gender identity and expression, and sex characteristics.

Sources: Asian Development Bank (South Asia Department); and C. March, I. Smyth, and M. Mukhopadhyay. 1999. *A Guide to Gender-Analysis Frameworks*. Oxford, United Kingdom: Oxfam GB.

APPENDIX 3: DETAILED CHECKLIST OF QUESTIONS FOR THREE AREAS OF GENDER EQUALITY AND SOCIAL INCLUSION ANALYSIS

Table A3.1: Detailed Checklist of Questions for Policy Makers and Service Providers

Level of Analysis	Indicative List of Questions
Policy analysis	1. Are there national or sector policies and action plans for women and excluded and vulnerable groups? 2. Do the policies (i) reflect an understanding of the needs and priorities of this group, (ii) aim to empower the group, (iii) aim to help in creating long-term attitudinal or institutional change, or (iv) seek to further discriminate against or formally exclude some groups of people or characteristics? 3. Do the policies consider the needs of people whose disadvantage is because of multiple and intersecting conditions and characteristics? 4. How have GESI policies been implemented? What is the operational guidance, and is it backed up with budget and staffing? 5. What new policy initiatives are being taken to address issues, and how are the different groups likely to benefit from them?
Institutional analysis	1. Where is the responsibility for GESI located in the organizational structure? Is there a key nodal ministry and department to address the needs of women and excluded and vulnerable groups at the national level? Is there a department within the sector agency to address the GESI issues? If yes, what are its mandates, roles, and primary responsibilities concerning the target group? 2. Are there GESI experts in the organization? What capacity development efforts were done to enhance the GESI capacity of the staff? 3. What is the level of diversity in staffing at different levels of the organization? Where are women and men, and people of disadvantaged groups located and in what positions, and who has access to information and decision-making authority?
Programming and budgeting	1. What is the budget allocation for (i) direct livelihood and voice empowerment of women and people of disadvantaged groups, (ii) supportive measures to develop an enabling environment, and (iii) reduction of discriminatory policies and practices? 2. How much of the GESI implementation (including specialized staff and subprojects) is funded by development partners' earmarked funds, and how much by the sector or institution's budget? 3. Does the organization collect and monitor data with disaggregation of its interventions and how the different target groups are affected by intersecting characteristics and conditions? 4. How are GESI aspects integrated into the monitoring and evaluation system (e.g., the monitoring and reporting templates, formats, and systems demand disaggregated data and analytical evidence about GESI issues)? 5. What are the project's innovations? What good practices and lessons could be used to improve the overall approach to GESI?

GESI = gender equality and social inclusion.

Source: Asian Development Bank (South Asia Department).

Table A3.2: Detailed Checklist of Questions for Other Stakeholders

Category of Stakeholder	Indicative List of Questions
Women and disadvantaged groups	1. What support have you received from the national government and sector agencies? 2. What types of schemes does the government have for women and excluded and vulnerable people? How do you know about the schemes, and how do you access the benefits (e.g., allowances or reservations in institutions or offices)? 3. Do you know of any national and sector policies that address gender-based violence? Have these enhanced your voice and decision-making ability? 4. What kind of training have you received to increase your skills? Have these training programs translated into better economic opportunities for you? 5. Have you been provided with suitable infrastructure in your area (e.g., roads, drinking water taps, toilets)? Who provided them? 6. Were you involved in any decision-making about the project-related policies? And how? 7. What are the key issues you experience in accessing services provided by state and sector projects because of your gender, age, disability, ethnicity or caste, SOGIESC, income status, and geographic location? 8. What is needed for women and excluded and vulnerable groups (e.g., those with disabilities, SOGIESC) to improve their quality of life? 9. How can things be improved to achieve women's empowerment and GESI? What can the government, development partners, and other stakeholder groups do for this?
All other stakeholders	1. What is the policy guidance from the national and sector agencies regarding these specific groups? How is it backed up with directives for appropriate budget and staffing? 2. To what extent have the directives and associated tools and processes focused evenly on the different categories of exclusion and vulnerability: (i) gender; (ii) disability, (iii) social identity (caste, ethnicity, and religion); (iv) sexual and gender identities; (v) geographical location; (vi) income status; (vii) old age; (viii) young age; and (ix) migrant status? 3. What institutional mechanisms are mandated to work for these categories? How well have they been resourced or staffed to perform their functions? 4. What have been their strengths and gaps in addressing the issues of the target groups? 5. How can things be improved to achieve women's empowerment and GESI? What can the government, development partners, and other stakeholder groups do for this?

GESI = gender equality and social inclusion; SOGIESC = sexual orientation, gender identity and expression, and sex characteristics.

Source: Asian Development Bank (South Asia Department).

APPENDIX 4: QUESTIONS FOR GENDER EQUALITY AND SOCIAL INCLUSION ANALYSIS OF RELEVANT NATIONAL LAWS, POLICIES, INSTITUTIONS, AND PROGRAMS RELATED TO ADB STRATEGY 2030 OPERATIONAL PRIORITIES 1 AND 2 AND INTERSECTIONALITY

Strategy 2030 OP1 and OP2 Pillars	Questions for GESI Analysis	
	Empower for Change	Include for Opportunity
OP1 (addressing remaining poverty and reducing inequalities)	1. What are the laws, policies, and/or programs in the country that aim to develop the capability of disadvantaged groups, such as older people, people with disabilities, excluded and vulnerable social identity groups (e.g., ethnic groups or castes, if any), people with diverse SOGIESC, income poor people, people in difficult geographic locations, and migrants, to access economic resources and opportunities, improve their livelihoods, participate in decision-making and governance, and respond to natural and human-induced disasters? 2. What are the achievements and gaps because of these policies and programs? What factors facilitated the achievements? What are the reasons for the gaps? 3. What are the related good practices of the government, international development agencies (including ADB), civil society organizations, and private business organizations?	1. Does the country have laws, policies, and/or programs that are meant to make public infrastructures; facilities, and services (e.g., energy, transport, water and sanitation, schools, health facilities, information and communication technology, market, finance); systems (e.g., representation in governance structures); social norms (educational curriculum, health services, social media); and public spaces and workplaces responsive to the inclusion needs of disadvantaged groups? 2. What are the informal rules and norms that govern the inclusiveness of operations of government and private service institutions? 3. What are the achievements and gaps of these laws, policies, and programs? What factors facilitated the achievements? What are the reasons for the gaps? 4. What are the related good practices of the government, international development agencies (including ADB), civil society organizations, and private business organizations?
OP2 (Accelerating progress in gender equality)	The same questions as OP1 but focused on women compared to men. What is the existing time poverty and drudgery experienced by women and girls (including those of different social groups)? What are the levels of gender-based violence experienced by women, girls, and people with diverse SOGIESC (especially those of disadvantaged groups), and what are the existing measures for protection?	The same questions as OP1 but focused on women and/or girls and individuals with diverse SOGIESC. In addition, what policies seek to discriminate against or formally exclude people based on their SOGIESC?
Intersectionality	The same questions as OP1 and OP2 but focused on women and/or girls, individuals with diverse SOGIESC, and men of disadvantaged groups experiencing intersecting inequalities.	The same questions as OP1 and OP2 but focused on women and/or girls, individuals with diverse SOGIESC, and men of disadvantaged groups experiencing intersecting inequalities.

ADB = Asian Development Bank; GESI= gender equality and social inclusion; OP1 = operational priority 1; OP2 = operational priority 2; SOGIESC = sexual orientation, gender identity and expression, and sexual characteristics

Note: The ADB Strategy 2030 OP2 focuses on gender equality and empowerment of women and girls, including those with diverse sexual orientation and gender identity and especially those experiencing intersecting inequalities due to their overlapping disadvantaged identities (e.g., old age, disability, social identity, income status, and geographic location). SARD, to be in sync with the laws and policies in four of its DMCs (Bangladesh, Bhutan, India, Nepal), has adopted a non-binary definition of gender identity encompassing people with diverse SOGIESC.

Source: Asian Development Bank (South Asia Department).

APPENDIX 5: DESCRIPTIVE AND TRANSFORMATIVE QUESTIONS OF INTERSECTIONALITY-BASED POLICY ANALYSIS FRAMEWORK

Type	No.	Questions for Policy Analysis
Descriptive	1	What knowledge, values, and experience do you (policy analysts) bring to this area of policy analysis?
	2	What is the policy "problem" under consideration? *(What problem[s] is the policy aiming to address?)*
	3	How have representations of the "problem" come about? *(What process was undertaken to identify and frame the problem[s]? Who were involved in identifying and framing the problem[s]?)*
	4	How are groups differentially affected by this representation of the "problem"? *(Who are the groups experiencing, or affected by, the problem[s]? Are women, men, people with diverse SOGIESC, especially those belonging to disadvantaged groups affected by the problem[s]? Were they involved in identifying and framing the problem[s]?*
	5	What are the current policy responses to the "problem"? *(What solutions does the policy offer to the problem?)*
Transformative	6	What inequities actually exist in relation to the "problem"?
	7	Where and how can interventions be made to improve *(the framing or understanding of)* the problem?
	8	What are feasible short, medium and long-term solutions *(to the problem[s])*?
	9	How will the proposed policy responses reduce inequities?
	10	How will implementation and uptake be assured?
	11	How will you know if inequities have been reduced?
	12	How has the process of engaging in an intersectionality-based policy analysis transformed the following? (i) Your thinking about relations and structures of power and inequity (ii) The ways in which you and others engage in the work of policy development, implementation, and evaluation (iii) Broader conceptualizations, relations, and effects of power asymmetry in the everyday world

SOGIESC = sexual orientation, gender identity and expression, and sex characteristics.

Note: Words in italics are interpretations of the questions and have been added to simplify the questions.

Source: O. Hankivsky et al. 2014. An intersectionality-based policy analysis framework: critical reflections on a methodology for advancing equity. *International Journal for Equity in Health*. 13 (119).

APPENDIX 6: QUESTIONS FOR GENDER EQUALITY AND SOCIAL INCLUSION ANALYSIS OF THE SITUATION OF WOMEN AND OTHER DISADVANTAGED GROUPS IN ADB'S SECTORS OF ENGAGEMENT

Table A6.1: Questions Relevant to All Sectors

Strategy 2030	Questions for GESI Analysis Across Sectors (Understand for Action)
OP1: addressing remaining poverty and reducing inequalities	1. What is the representation of people of disadvantaged groups, e.g., people with disabilities, minority ethnic groups or castes (if any), and people with diverse SOGIESC, compared to people with no disabilities, other ethnic groups, and people whose SOGIESC is consistent with their sex assigned at birth, in the leadership and management and rank-and-file staff of government agencies, private organizations, and civil society organizations in each sector? 2. What are the major types of employment in the sector? What proportion of the owners or managers and workers/staff are members of disadvantaged groups in these occupations or sectors? 3. What barriers do older people, people with disabilities, identity groups, and people with diverse SOGIESC experience (compared to people with no disabilities, other ethnic groups, and people whose SOGIESC is consistent with their sex assigned at birth) in accessing the services, resources, and opportunities (including employment) in the sector at the interpersonal, family/household, community, institution, and policy levels? 4. What have been the adverse effects of these barriers to their personal development and the development of their families, community, and sector? 5. What role do social norms play in creating barriers to GESI for women and men of disadvantaged groups across sectors? 6. What is the management information system of government sector agencies and relevant private organizations to capture the situation of disadvantaged groups in the sector?
OP 2: accelerating progress in gender equality	The same questions as OP1 but focused on women compared to men. What role do men play in creating, sustaining, or removing the barriers to gender equality? What is the existing time poverty and drudgery experienced by women and girls (including those of different social groups)? What are the levels of gender-based violence experienced by women and girls (especially those of disadvantaged groups) and people with diverse SOGIESC, and what are the existing measures for protection?
Intersectionality and common to OP1 and OP2	The same questions as OP1 and OP2 but focused on women, people with diverse SOGIESC, and men experiencing intersecting inequalities. What role do social and gender norms play in creating barriers to GESI for women and other disadvantaged groups across sectors? What is the role of men and masculinity in creating and sustaining these barriers?

GESI = gender equality and social inclusion; OP1 = operational priority 1; OP2 = operational priority 2; SOGIESC = sexual orientation, gender identity and expression, and sexual characteristics

Source: Asian Development Bank (South Asia Department).

Table A6.2: Questions for Specific Sectors for Country Partnership Strategy and Program or Project Gender Equality and Social Inclusion Design Features

Sector	Questions for GESI Analysis of Specific Sectors
Agriculture, natural resources, and rural development	1. What proportion of women, men, individuals with diverse SOGIESC, older people, people with disability, and members of excluded and vulnerable ethnic groups or castes are absentee landowners, land owner-cultivators, or landless agricultural workers? 2. How does their land tenure situation affect their access to water resources, including irrigation, and participation in the management of water resources? 3. How do the systems for land titling, land registration, land valuation, land taxation, and land dispute resolution secure the land tenure rights of women and other disadvantaged groups? 4. What is the access of women, individuals with diverse SOGIESC, and members of other disadvantaged groups to production inputs such as seeds, fertilizer, and capital? 5. Are women, individuals with diverse SOGIESC, and members of other disadvantaged groups visible (i.e., have access to and control over resources) in each stage of the agriculture value chain (for specific major crops in the country)? If yes, what is their form and level of participation in every stage? If no, what are the barriers? 6. Are there formal or customary laws, policies, and programs that promote (i) the building of resilience of women, men, individuals with diverse SOGIESC, older people, people with disability, and members of disadvantaged ethnic groups or castes to climate change and disaster impacts in rural areas; and (ii) inclusive climate-smart agriculture and sustainable land use? 7. What are the implications of feminization of agriculture on women, and what future measures are required to reduce negative results and build on any potential positive aspects? 8. How do the systems for access to and control of forests secure the rights of women and other disadvantaged groups?
Education	9. Are there laws, policies, and programs that promote a system-wide education transformation to benefit all learners equally, regardless of gender, disabilities, social affiliation, income status, and geographic location? If yes, what are they? If there are none, what has constrained the government from initiating the development of these laws, policies, and programs? 10. Are there laws, policies, and programs that promote inclusive education in terms of equal access to ensure that (i) girls and women, individuals with diverse SOGIESC, and members of disadvantaged groups with and without disabilities participate and excel in fields traditionally associated with boys and men; and (ii) boys and men with and without disabilities can choose to enter into fields associated with girls and women without prejudice? If yes, what are they? If none, what has constrained the government from initiating the development of these laws, policies, and programs? 11. What opportunities do women and adolescent girls have in STEM disciplines to promote nontraditional and higher-paying jobs?
Energy	12. What proportions of households that (i) are headed by women and individuals with diverse SOGIESC; (ii) have members that have disabilities (because of old age and physical, sensory, and mental disabilities); (iii) are income poor; and (iv) are of disadvantaged ethnic groups or castes have access to a stable power supply? 13. Are there laws, policies, and programs that promote the equal involvement of women, men, individuals with diverse SOGIESC, people with disability, and members of different ethnic groups or castes in the generation, transmission, and distribution of renewable energy through viable economic enterprises? If yes, what are they? If there are none, what has constrained the government from initiating the development of these laws, policies, and programs? 14. What are the traditional fuel-gathering tasks of rural women, and what measures exist to improve access to affordable, modern, and clean energy to ease unpaid care and domestic work responsibilities?
Finance	15. Are there laws, policies, and programs that (i) promote the engagement of women and excluded and vulnerable groups in micro, small, and medium-sized enterprises; or (ii) make it possible for these groups to start businesses and, as entrepreneurs, be able to access resources and services from financing institutions and investors? If yes, what are they? What have been their outcomes? What are the challenges? 16. How many women-led or women-owned MSMEs exist? What are the women-relevant financial technology and women-friendly finance products and services?

continued on next page

Table A6.2 continued

Sector	Questions for GESI Analysis of Specific Sectors
Health	17. What are the barriers (e.g., financial and transportation) to access affordable quality health services experienced by excluded and vulnerable groups, especially by women, given their reproductive and maternal health needs and their traditional responsibility for the family's health needs? What role do men play? What enabling role do men play? 18. What are the different care service modalities for young children, older people, and persons with severe disabilities in the country or program or project areas? 19. What are the maternal mortality ratio, early pregnancy rate, child marriage rate, and sex-selective abortion rate? What are the priorities for women's sexual and reproductive health and rights and for reducing gender-based violence? 20. Are there specific and inclusive health services provided to fit the unique needs of LGBTQI+ people and those with diverse SOGIESC? Do health policies discriminate against (healthy) intersex babies and enforce medically unnecessary surgeries on their bodies?
Industry and trade	21. What proportion of businesses in the industrial corridor are owned or managed by women, individuals with diverse SOGIESC, older people, people with disability, and members of excluded and vulnerable ethnic groups or castes? 22. Are there laws, policies, and programs that promote the engagement of women and excluded and vulnerable groups in businesses in the industrial corridor? If yes, what are they? If there are none, what has constrained the government from initiating the development of these laws, policies, and programs? 23. What are the opportunities for women to participate effectively and to increase their role in trade and industry sectors? What gender-specific barriers constrain women's increased role in these sectors?
Public sector management	24. In what parts of public administration are women and excluded and vulnerable groups concentrated (e.g., health and education for women) and less represented (e.g., defense, public works, and transportation for women)? 25. Are there laws, policies, and programs that promote the engagement of women and excluded and vulnerable groups in public sector management? If yes, what are they? If there are none, what has constrained the government from initiating the development of these laws, policies, and programs? 26. Is there a gender-responsive budgeting system in the country? How effective has it been in tracking the budgets spent on women's empowerment and gender equality and the investment results?
Transport	27. Are the transport infrastructure design and services sensitive to the mobility and safety needs of the elderly, people with disability, women, and children? If yes, what are these transport designs and services? What are the factors that have facilitated their presence? If no, what are the constraints? 28. What are the barriers to the safe mobility of women and excluded and vulnerable groups? 29. What are semi-skilled and skilled employment opportunities for women in urban and rural transport sectors? What measures are taken to prevent sexual harassment, exploitation and abuse, and other social risks during construction?
Water and other urban infrastructure and services	30. Are there laws, policies, and programs that promote equality in housing tenure rights and inclusive access to basic services (water, sanitation, health, and education facilities) of women and excluded and vulnerable groups in poor urban communities? If yes, what are they? What have been their outcomes? If there are none, what has constrained the government from initiating the development of these laws, policies, and programs? 31. How much time do women and girls spend collecting water, and what measures are taken for managing menstrual hygiene? How is urban development designed to address women's requirements?

GESI = gender equality and social inclusion; LGBTQI+ = lesbian, gay, bisexual, transgender, queer, intersex, and others; SOGIESC = sexual orientation, gender identity and expression, and sexual characteristics.

Source: Asian Development Bank (South Asia Department).

APPENDIX 7: KEY QUESTIONS FOR THE GENDER EQUALITY AND SOCIAL INCLUSION ANALYSIS OF SECTOR LAWS, POLICIES, INSTITUTIONS, AND PROGRAMS

Strategy 2030 OP1 and OP2	Questions for GESI Analysis	
	Empower for Change	Include for Opportunity
OP1 (addressing remaining poverty and reducing inequalities) pillars: 1. Human capital and social protection enhanced for all 2. Quality jobs generated 3. Opportunities for the most vulnerable increased	1. Are the sector agencies and relevant private entities mandated to observe sector-specific laws, policies, and programs designed to ensure (i) access to sector services, resources, programs, information, and opportunities; and (ii) participation in consultations and collaborative work of disadvantaged groups, particularly older people, people with disabilities, people with diverse SOGIESC, excluded and vulnerable social identity groups (e.g., ethnic groups or castes), disadvantaged youth, income poor, and people in remote geographic locations? If yes, what are these laws, policies, and programs? Do the sector agencies and private entities observe them? If yes, to what extent? 2. What have been the effects of these efforts of sector agencies and private entities on the economic, voice, and social empowerment of these disadvantaged groups? 3. If there are none, what has constrained the government from formulating these laws, policies, and programs?	Given the answers to question 1 under "empower for change," what is the overall analysis of the following sector systems and structures? 1. Affordability, accessibility, and responsiveness of services to disadvantaged groups 2. Accessibility of resources, including offices and other infrastructures 3. Accessibility of information and communication systems 4. Responsiveness of human resource management and operational systems to disadvantaged groups (for internal officers, managers, and staff) 5. Capability of the database management system to capture and provide GESI information 6. Inclusiveness of grievance redress mechanisms
OP2 (accelerating progress in gender equality)	The same questions as OP1 but focused on women and girls. What is the level of representation of women in the organization, and at which levels? What are the organizational policies to provide them with a supporting environment?	The same questions as OP1 but focused on women and individuals with diverse SOGIESC
Intersectionality	The same questions as OP1 but focused on women and individuals with diverse SOGIESC who are experiencing intersecting inequalities	The same questions as OP1 but focused on women and individuals with diverse SOGIESC experiencing intersecting inequalities

GESI = gender equality and social inclusion; OP1 = operational priority 1; OP2 = operational priority2; SOGIESC = sexual orientation, gender identity and expression, and sexual characteristics.

Source: Asian Development Bank (South Asia Department).

APPENDIX 8: EXAMPLES OF QUESTIONS ON GOOD PRACTICES OF DEVELOPMENT PARTNERS

1. What work has your agency been doing on the different categories of exclusion and vulnerability? These categories include (i) gender; (ii) disability, (iii) social identity (caste, ethnicity, and religion); (iv) SOGIESC; (v) geographical location; (vi) income status; (vii) old age; (viii) young age; and (ix) migrant status.
2. Does your organization support people negatively affected by intersecting factors and characteristics? Which ones, and how?
3. What have been the key successes and the key challenges? What factors have supported or constrained your work with women and with the different excluded and vulnerable groups?
4. Which activities have seemed most helpful to the target disadvantaged group?
5. What has supported persons (with disaggregation) within these groups to access services, influence decisions or discuss issues with decision-makers, and reduce discriminatory practices and norms? What is required for things to improve in the future?
6. How does M&E capture gender and inclusion issues? What is well monitored and what is not, and how? What changes have occurred in the lives of women and excluded and vulnerable groups? How did these happen, and were they because of the interventions of agencies (e.g., donors, development partners, civil society)? What else is required? As there are limited M&E and impact evaluations on programs for people with diverse SOGIESC, does your agency plan or is your agency open to engage in these M&E and impact evaluations?
7. What good practices and lessons exist regarding enhancing livelihood and voice empowerment and changing discriminatory policies and mindsets for each of the excluded and vulnerable groups?
8. What have been your experiences and learnings from projects aimed at providing basic services (like health, education, sanitation, clean drinking water, information and communication technology, mobile, banking services, and quality jobs) to different groups?
9. How have skill training programs been provided to these groups to enhance their economic opportunities?
10. How have your programs reduced time poverty for women and the income poor?
11. How have your programs strengthened women's and the disadvantaged groups' decision-making and participation at the community and policy-making levels? Can you share your experience in designing and implementing programs to enhance their resilience to external shocks like climate change?
12. Share the details of each good practice (content, design, implementation, and outcomes of the practice). Why is it considered a good practice? What methods and tools were used, and why were they effective? How did the intervention benefit the specific excluded or vulnerable group? How was it disseminated? How can its achievements be followed up and scaled up?
13. What are the key lessons? What was done well, and what needed improvement?
14. What initiatives have been taken to prevent, reduce, and respond to gender-based violence.

M&E = monitoring and evaluation, SOGIESC = sexual orientation, gender identity and expressions, and sex characteristics.

Source: Asian Development Bank (South Asia Department).

APPENDIX 9: QUESTIONS FOR GENDER EQUALITY AND SOCIAL INCLUSION ANALYSIS FOR PROGRAM AND PROJECT GENDER EQUALITY AND SOCIAL INCLUSION DESIGN FEATURES

Strategy 2030 OP1 and OP2	Questions for GESI Analysis		
	Understand for Action	Empower for Change	Include for Opportunity
OP1 (addressing remaining poverty and reducing inequalities)	1. What disadvantaged groups (e.g., older people, disadvantaged youth, people with disabilities, excluded and vulnerable social identity groups, people with diverse SOGIESC, income poor people, and people in difficult geographic locations) can benefit or be affected by the program or project? 2. What poverty, social exclusion, and vulnerability issues do these disadvantaged groups experience?	1. What services related to the program or project can contribute to the disadvantaged group's economic, voice, and social empowerment? 2. Are there barriers to the disadvantaged groups' current access to these services? If yes, what are they?	1. What policies, organizations, procedures, and infrastructures in the program or project areas are related to the program or project objectives? 2. Are these policies, organizations, procedures, and infrastructures inclusive or do they contribute to the inclusion of the disadvantaged groups? What are their strengths and limitations related to the promotion of inclusion for opportunities of disadvantaged groups?
OP2 (accelerating progress in gender equality)	1. What is the population of women, men, girls, boys, and individuals with diverse SOGIESC in the program or project areas? 2. What program or project-related gender inequality issues do they experience?	1. What program or project services can contribute to the economic, voice, and social empowerment of women and/or girls and individuals with diverse SOGIESC? 2. Are there barriers to their current access to these services? If yes, what are they?	1. What masculinity issues and other factors keep men, families, and communities from recognizing the equality and inclusion rights of women, girls, and individuals with diverse SOGIESC? 2. Do the current policies, organizations, procedures, and infrastructures relevant to the program or project promote gender equality?
Intersectionality	1. In the program or project areas, what proportion of each disadvantaged group (mentioned in OP1) are women, girls, and individuals with diverse SOGIESC? 2. What GESI issues do they experience compared to men and boys of disadvantaged groups and women and girls of advantaged groups? 3. What are the social issues faced by men and boys experiencing intersecting inequalities?	Do women, girls, and individuals with diverse SOGIESC experience distinct barriers to accessing program- or project-related services that can contribute to their economic, voice, and social empowerment? If yes, what are they?	1. Are current policies, organizations, procedures, and infrastructures relevant to the program or project designed to respond to the distinct needs of women, girls, men, boys, and individuals with diverse SOGIESC experiencing intersecting inequalities? If yes, what are the responses? If not, what are the constraints?

GESI = gender equality and social inclusion; OP1 = operational priority 1; OP2 = operational priority 2; SOGIESC = sexual orientation, gender identity and expression, and sexual characteristics.

Source: Asian Development Bank (South Asia Department).

APPENDIX 10: DETAILED CHECKLIST OF QUESTIONS FOR SITUATIONAL ANALYSIS ADDRESSED TO SPECIFIC STAKEHOLDERS

Category of Stakeholders	Indicative List of Questions
All (except beneficiary group with whom discussion will be separate)	1. What are the different groups in the program area (with respect to caste, ethnicity, age, disability, and other dimensions)? What is their population, disaggregated by gender, social identity, age, disability, and other relevant variables? 2. Which groups of people experience exclusion and vulnerability in the country? Who has control over what resources? 3. Which social groups within the country have better human development indicators than others? And why? 4. Which groups within the country have the poorest human development indicators? Is this because of personal and social characteristics that intersect with each? If so, which characteristics? Are these characteristics related to their (i) gender; (ii) disability; (iii) social identity (caste, ethnicity, and religion); (iv) SOGIESC; (v) geographical location; (vi) income status; (vii) old age; (viii) young age; and (ix) migrant status? 5. What is the level of access to basic services (like health, education, sanitation, clean drinking water, clean fuel, ICT, mobile, and banking services) for each of these groups (mentioned in answer to question #4)? 6. What barriers does each of these groups experience in improving their (i) assets and capabilities (i.e., health, education, income-earning capacity); (ii) voice and ability to influence decisions; and (iii) ability to make service providers accountable (i.e., ability to claim rights and question service providers for accountability). 7. In what economic activities does each group primarily engage? What are the economic activities available to this group? What is the quality of such opportunities? 8. What barriers exist for women and other excluded and vulnerable groups in terms of skill levels, mobility, and social norms? 9. What is the dominant gender or social division of labor? 10. What are the specific discriminatory social practices that each of these groups experiences at the family and community levels and in accessing services provided by the state and projects? 11. What is the status of the representation of this group in different decision-making forums at the subnational and national levels? 12. Who are the key stakeholders in the ecosystem of the target beneficiaries, and who are the people likely to be adversely affected by the project? How can they be engaged in the project?
Beneficiary group	1. Do you have easy access to basic services (like health, education, sanitation, clean drinking water, ICT, mobile, and banking services)? 2. Are there any barriers you experience while accessing these services? What are these barriers? And what do you think are the reasons for these barriers? 3. What are your employment options, and what barriers exist for you in terms of skill levels, mobility, and social norms? If already in employment, what are the conditions? 4. Are efforts made to include you in decision-making forums at the national and subnational levels? 5. What behavior in families, communities, and offices that you experience is different from the behavior toward other groups who are considered advantaged? 6. How are tasks carried out within and outside the home by household members divided? Who does what? And what are the consequences of this division? Conduct a gender relations mapping. Identify relevant sectoral and empowerment-related indicators. Facilitate a discussion amongst participants (either sex/gender-disaggregated or mixed depending on the prevalent norms) to identify what is the existing pattern of division of labor, access to resources, and decision-making authority between women and men, i.e., who does the labor, has access, who makes the final decision, who has some influence on the decisions (as relevant for reach indicator); the first step is to discuss about the prevalent general practice in the settlement/community, then at the end of the discussion, whether there are caste/ethnic/religious differences, if yes what and then also ask about income differences.

ICT = information and communication technology.

Source: Asian Development Bank (South Asia Department).

Category of Stakeholder	Members Included
Policy makers	This category includes government ministries, concerned departments, or agencies appointed specifically to address GESI issues at the national and subnational levels. This group of stakeholders has decision-making power, and consultations with them will help formulate a deep understanding of the institutional and policy issues related to GESI.
Target groups	This category includes identified disadvantaged women and excluded and vulnerable groups in each country to provide them the space to voice their barriers and priorities. It is important to also engage men and boys in GESI programs.
CSOs	ADB defines CSOs as nonprofit organizations independent from the government, which operate around common interests. They vary in size, interests, and function, and include NGOs, youth groups, community-based organizations, independent academic and research institutes, professional associations, foundations, faith-based organizations, people's organizations, and labor unions.[a]
International agencies	This category includes organizations, such as the Foreign, Commonwealth and Development Office of the Government of the United Kingdom, United Nations and its specialized agencies, funds, and programs (including UNDP, UNICEF, UNFPA, UN Women, and the ILO); USAID; the World Bank; and international NGOs, such as CARE International, Humanity & Inclusion, Plan International, Save the Children, SNV, that are present in the target countries and have identified GESI as a priority area for their interventions in SARD DMCs.
Key resource persons	This category includes key informants such as subject matter experts and/or technical experts dedicated to issues related to GESI. This includes members of leading universities and/or research organizations engaged in innovative research activities to address GESI issues.
ADB officials	This includes ADB project staff, GESI teams, and officials at headquarters and country resident missions in the respective SARD DMCs. Consultations with them will focus on ADB's agenda for mainstreaming GESI in the target geographies and the specific sectors, good practices and lessons from previous projects, and insights on GESI mainstreaming in SARD operations.

ADB = Asian Development Bank, CSO = civil society organization, DFID = Department for International Development of the United Kingdom, DMC = developing member country, GESI = gender equality and social inclusion, ILO = International Labour Organization, NGO = nongovernment organization, SARD = South Asia Department, UNDP = United Nations Development Programme, UNFPA = United Nations Population Fund, UNICEF = United Nations Children's Fund, UN Women = United Nations Entity for Gender Equality and the Empowerment of Women, USAID = United States Agency for International Development.Note: This table contains the possible stakeholders for key informant interviews, consultation meetings, and focus groups discussion. In all these stakeholder groups, it is important to ensure the significant representation of women; men; individuals with diverse sexual orientation, gender identity and expression, and sexual characteristics; and representatives of other relevant social groups categorized, for example, by age, ethnic group or caste, class, and disability.

[a] ADB. 2021. Promotion of Engagement with Civil Society Organizations. *Operations Manual.* OM E4. Manila.

Source: Asian Development Bank (SARD).